D1757517

Wayne's Wedding

Wayne's Wedding

John Escott

Illustrated by Jacqui Thomas

A Blackie Bear

British Library Cataloguing in Publication Data
Escott, John
Wayne's wedding.—(A Blackie Bear)
I. Title   II. Thomas, Jacqui
823'914[J]   PZ7

ISBN 0-216-92402-2

Blackie and Son Limited
7 Leicester Place, London WC2H 7BP

Printed in Great Britain by
Thomson Litho Ltd, East Kilbride, Scotland

About the Author

John Escott has written more than twenty-five books for children under ten, among them *A Walk Down the Pier*, *Alarm Bells*, *Burglar Bells* and the popular *Radio* series about a group of children running a children's local radio programme. He writes a weekly comic script for a young children's magazine and has also written numerous short stories for children's magazines. *Wayne's Wedding* is soon to be followed by the further adventures of Wayne and his big sister Gemma in *Wayne's Luck*. John Escott is married, has two children and lives in Bournemouth.

Wayne is my brother. He is five years old and I am nearly seven.

'Keep an eye on Wayne, Gemma,' Mum is always saying. 'You know what he's like.'

I do know what he's like. Everybody knows what Wayne is like. If they don't, they should have come to THE WEDDING and then they would have found out.

It's funny but I always think of THE WEDDING in big letters. It must be because of all the things that happened.

I'll tell you about them...

It was a Saturday morning. We were all having breakfast when Mum broke the news.

'Patsy Millar is getting married next Saturday,' she said. 'We are all going to the wedding.'

Wayne made a face.

'Weddings are boring,' he said.

'You've never been to one

before, so how do you know?' I said.

Wayne didn't answer. He just screwed up his nose. He was probably thinking of Patsy Millar. She was the daughter of Dad's boss, Mr Millar. She was tall and skinny with huge teeth.

'Anyway,' said Mum. 'You have to come to the wedding, and that's that. Gran will be away that day and there's nobody else to look after you. Gemma will keep an eye on you.'

Mum said this in her don't-you-dare-argue voice.

It was the first wedding I had been to. In fact, I'd begun to think nobody was ever going to invite me to one and that I wouldn't know what to do at my own.

Wayne hates going anywhere if it means dressing up. He hates it only slightly less than having his hair washed.

'I feel like a Christmas parcel!'
he wailed the following
Saturday morning. Mum had
forced him to dress in itchy-new
trousers, squeaky-new shoes, a
pink shirt and a pink tie.

I had a new strawberry
coloured dress and shoes. Mum
looked at both of us and nodded.

'You'll do,' she said.

Wayne had kicked up such a fuss about being made tidy, we were late getting to the church. He always makes us late getting to places. It makes me mad!

The Vicar was in the church porch waiting for Patsy Millar to arrive.

'I'm so sorry we're late,' Mum said, as she and I ran up the church steps.

Dad was still pulling Wayne out of the car.

'The bride is late as well,' said the Vicar, 'so you're all right.'

'I want to sit in the front row,' Wayne said when Dad dragged him to the church door.

'You can't,' Dad said. 'That's

for the bride's family. We shall sit at the back.'

'But I shan't be able to see what happens!' Wayne cried.

'You didn't want to come anyway,' I reminded him.

He just scowled at me.

The Vicar tried to put things right. 'How would you like to sit next to my wife?' he said. 'She plays the organ. You'll be able to see everything from up there.'

'Go with him, Gemma,' Mum said, as Wayne rushed off down the aisle before anybody could argue. 'Keep an eye on him.'

How many eyes was I supposed to have, I wondered as I hurried after Wayne.

The church was full. Ladies
wearing large hats gave us
peculiar looks as we trotted
towards the organ at the side of
the altar.

'Hallo,' said the Vicar's wife, smiling. She didn't seem to mind having company.

Not at first, anyway.

Not until Wayne slipped off the organ stool and put his feet on the pedals.

BLAAAAGH! went the organ,

just as Patsy Millar, looking much prettier than I remembered her, reached the altar.

Patsy gave a little scream and dropped her flowers.

'Sorry!' Wayne shouted across to her as he scrambled back up on to the stool with a couple more BLAAAGH-BLAAAGHs!

'Shut up!' I hissed at him.

After that, the Vicar's wife made several mistakes. Just having Wayne near seemed to make her nervous. He does that to people, I've noticed.

After the service, the photographer took pictures of the bride and bridegroom outside the church. Then he took pictures of some of the guests. Wayne ran around after the photographer and got into four of the pictures before I spotted him and dragged him away.

'They don't want you to remind them of their wedding day,' I told him. 'Although after that terrible noise you made on the organ, they're not likely to forget you.'

'I just slipped,' Wayne said. 'After that, the organ lady played lots of wrong notes.'

'You're enough to make anyone play wrong notes!' I said.

Soon Dad and Mum came over. 'Come on,' Dad said. 'Let's drive to the reception.'

'Reception?' Wayne said. 'What's that?'

'The eating and drinking bit,' Dad said.

'Oh,' Wayne said, smiling. 'That sounds better.'

The wedding reception was at the biggest and poshest hotel in the town. Wayne went round five times in the revolving door before Dad yanked him inside.

We went into a small room
where the wedding presents were
spread out on a huge table.

'Where's the food?' Wayne
asked.

'Shh!' I said. 'Just wait, will you? Look at the lovely presents.'

Wayne stared at an ugly-looking cuckoo clock.

'I hope nobody gives me one of those when I get married,' he said in a loud voice.

Several people looked at Wayne as if he was something nasty that had crawled out from under the skirting board.

The meal was served in a much larger room with a stage at one end. We all sat down and had a chicken salad and some sort of gooey pink mixture afterwards. And a piece of wedding cake so small that Wayne asked a waitress for another slice.

'You can't have any more,' I whispered to him. 'Everybody gets just one piece.'

But, would you believe it, the waitress brought him some more! Then she disappeared

before I had a chance to ask for
another slice.

The speeches came next. The
bride's father began by saying
what a wonderful girl Patsy was
and how he would miss her.

I stared out of the window. There was a swimming pool in the garden of the hotel. It was shaped like a heart and the blue water shone in the sun. Sunbeds and deckchairs were spread about the lawn but nobody was around.

I closed my eyes and imagined myself jumping into the lovely cool, blue water. Away from the stuffy room and the boring voices.

When I opened my eyes, Wayne was no longer sitting beside me.

I looked up and down the room.

At the stage.

Under the table.

No Wayne.

Mum and Dad were so busy listening to the speeches, they didn't notice that Wayne had disappeared.

I looked out into the garden again.

And saw Wayne taking off all his clothes.

His itchy-new trousers, his squeaky-new shoes, his pink tie, his pink shirt, his pants and socks.

Then he walked down into the blue swimming pool!

Wayne loves swimming. He goes to the baths each week and doesn't need arm bands or a rubber ring.

I watched him now, floating on his back, splashing his feet up and down. He was having a very good time.

But I had to do something. And quickly, before somebody noticed him. Otherwise I'd be in

trouble. 'Keep an eye on him,' Mum had said.

Getting up very quietly, I crept out through an open patio door and ran down towards the pool.

'Wayne!' I called.

Wayne didn't seem to hear.

Or he pretended not to.

'Wayne!' I called again.

'Shall I fetch a towel, miss?' said a voice from behind me.

It was a hotel waitress. The one who had given Wayne the extra slice of wedding cake.

'Er—thank you. He's—er—my brother,' I explained.

The waitress smiled. 'He seems to be enjoying himself,' she said. Then she went to fetch the towel.

Enjoying himself! 'Wayne!' I yelled. 'Get out of that pool at once!'

Wayne blew bubbles across the water. He didn't look surprised to see me.

'You should come in too,

Gemma,' he said. 'It's lovely.'

The waitress arrived back with a huge fluffy white towel. The name of the hotel was printed on one side. It looked big enough for two Waynes. She handed it to me, trying not to laugh, and then went away.

'Come on in, Gem,' Wayne shouted.

I whirled round. 'You come OUT!' I told him, in a voice that sounded so much like Mum's it startled me.

And it worked.

'Oh, all right,' Wayne grumbled, and he walked up out of the water on to the blue tiles around the pool.

He was looking over my shoulder at something. I turned to see what it was.

Mum's shocked face stared through the window. Her nose was pressed against the glass. She looked as if she had seen a ghost.

There were other noses pressed against the glass as well.

Wayne smiled and gave them all a wave before taking the fluffy white towel.

'Wayne!' Mum burst out of the door and ran towards the pool. 'Gemma! What on earth...?'

'I've had a lovely swim,' Wayne said, wiping himself dry.

I was opening and shutting my mouth, trying to think of something to say.

'Swim indeed!' Mum was furious. She snatched the towel and bundled Wayne into his clothes. 'Why didn't you keep an eye on him, Gemma? I've never been so embarrassed in all my life. What will all those people think? What will Mr Millar think? What—?'

Then an awful thing happened.

Mum stepped back on to some wet tiles beside the pool and slipped. 'Aaagh!' she cried, as she fell into the water with a huge SPLASH!

I closed my eyes. It's
something I often do when
trouble is on the way. When I
opened them again, we were in
the middle of a crowd. All the
other guests had come into the
garden. Dad had rolled up his
trousers and was wading out
towards Mum.

Suddenly, Mrs Millar, the bride's mother, grabbed Wayne by the arm and started to drag him towards the hotel. 'Come with me!' she shrieked. 'You too, Gemma.'

I followed. It seemed the best thing to do. Anyway, I didn't want to be around when Mum came out of the water.

Mrs Millar stamped along the hallway and opened a door. It was the room where all the wedding presents were spread out.

'Wait in here,' she told us. 'And DON'T TOUCH ANYTHING.' Her face was red and she looked as if she wanted to strangle Wayne. Well, she will have to join a queue, I thought.

CUCKOO! went the ugly cuckoo clock as Mrs Millar left the room.

I gave a big sigh. 'What a wedding this is turning out to be,' I said.

'What's the matter?' Wayne said, looking all innocent. 'I'm enjoying it.'

'It's all right for you,' I said. 'Mum and Dad will go mad when we get home and I'll get ticked off. It isn't fair.'

Wayne stared at the wedding presents, screwing up his nose. The table was covered with a large white tablecloth which hung over the front, reaching to the floor.

A smile spread slowly across Wayne's face. Then, quick as a flash, he ducked down and crawled under the table.

'Wayne, come out,' I said in my stern voice.

He didn't come out.

'Stop messing about and come out!' I said in a louder voice.

A lump appeared in the tablecloth and I could hear Wayne snorting with laughter.

'I'll come and get you,' I threatened.

More snorting.

'Right then.' I dropped onto my hands and knees and dived into the darkness beneath the tablecloth.

As I did so, somebody came into the room.

We both knelt there and held our breath. Then I lifted the edge of the tablecloth.

A pair of legs in green trousers stood very close to my nose.

The next thing we heard was something being taken from the table top. Were they packing up the presents ready to go? If so, the tablecloth would be whisked off very soon.

Then the green-trousered legs moved away.

Quickly.

And on tiptoe.

Something was wrong, I knew

it was. I lifted the cloth a teeny
bit higher—and my heart
jumped!

A hotel porter in his green
uniform had the cuckoo clock
under one arm. He was peering
into the hall to see if anybody
was about.

He's stealing it! The words screamed silently inside my head and I dropped the tablecloth to the floor again.

'What's happening?' Wayne asked in a low voice.

I told him in a whisper.

'A THIEF!' he yelled and, without thinking, he stood up and banged his head. 'OW!'

He tried to get out from under the table and became hopelessly tangled up in the white cloth.

It must have frightened the porter half to death, which was hardly surprising. All the man saw was a white tablecloth with a pair of moving bumps under it. And all he heard were

Wayne's blood-curdling howls as he rubbed his sore head.

Anyway, the porter dropped the cuckoo clock as if it was a lump of hot coal.

COOO-CUCK! COOO-CUCK! COOO-CUCK!

I peered out from under the tablecloth in time to see a small bird bursting out of the front of the clock and some important looking springs falling out of the back. COOO-CUCK! COOO-CUCK! COOO-CUCK! On and on went the noise. The clock seemed to have gone crazy.

People ran in to see what was happening. One of them was the Hotel Manager.

He saw a white-faced porter pressed against the door frame, watching the ghostly, moving tablecloth where Wayne was still trying to get out. He also saw the cuckoo clock and quickly realized what had happened.

'Why, you thieving—!'

The rest of the Manager's words were drowned in an even louder COOOOOO-CUCK! before the clock shuddered into silence.

Wayne and I crawled out from under the table.

'What's happening now?' Mrs Millar wailed.

'I think these two young people have stopped a thief stealing your daughter's wedding presents,' the Hotel Manager told her. He put a firm hand on the porter's arm.

Mum and Dad were at the front of the crowd, their mouths open like trap doors. Mum's dress was making a puddle of water around her feet.

'Well done, you two,' the Hotel Manager went on, smiling at Wayne and me. 'Who knows what else this thief might have taken if you hadn't been clever enough to frighten him.'

Wayne grinned and looked pleased with himself.

I just felt sick.

'Er—I think it's time we went home,' Dad said, stepping forward and taking hold of Wayne's hand.

'Oh, must you go?' said the Manager.

'Yes, we must,' Dad said.

'Definitely,' Mum said, dripping into her puddle.

While we were driving home in the car, I decided I probably wouldn't get married when I grew up. At least, if I did, I would not have a big wedding.

Or if I did have a big wedding, I would NOT invite my brother Wayne.

After all, who would keep an eye on him?

Would you?